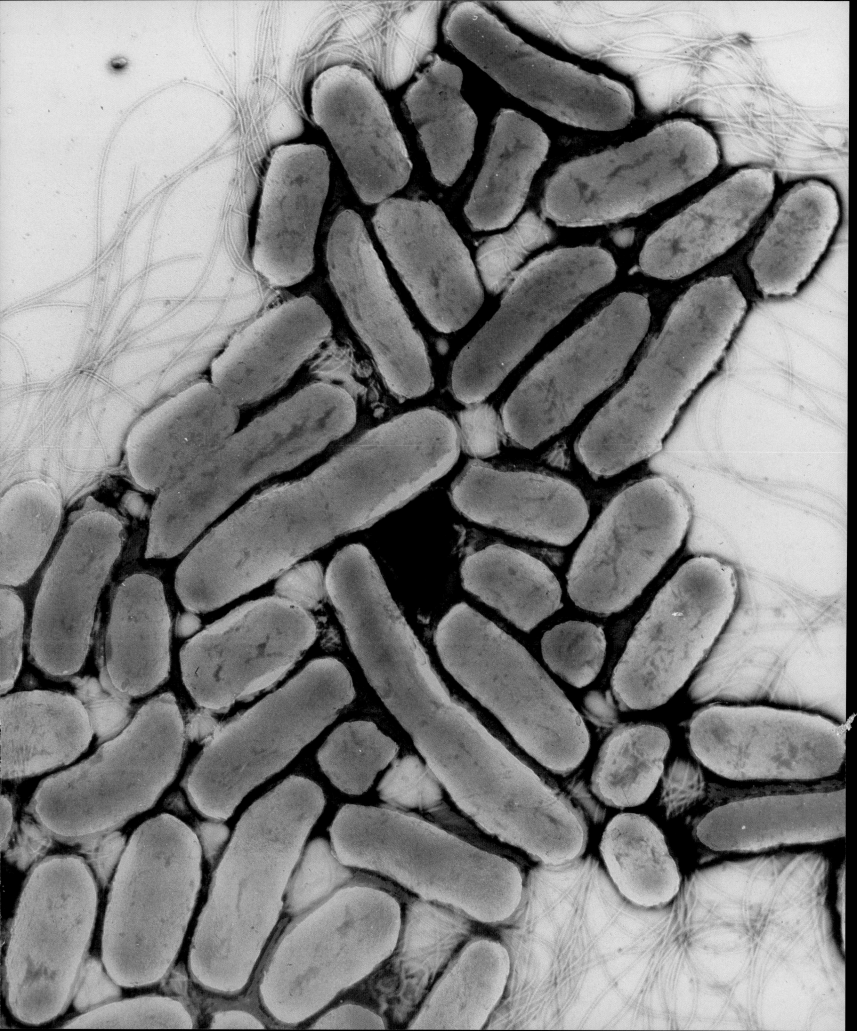

BACTERIA

B. ELLEN FRIEDMAN

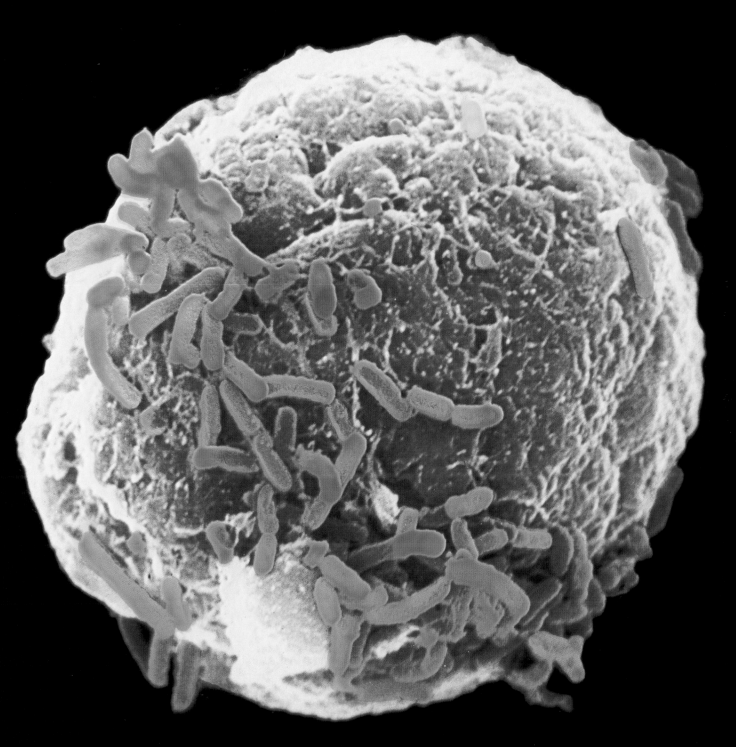

CREATIVE EDUCATION

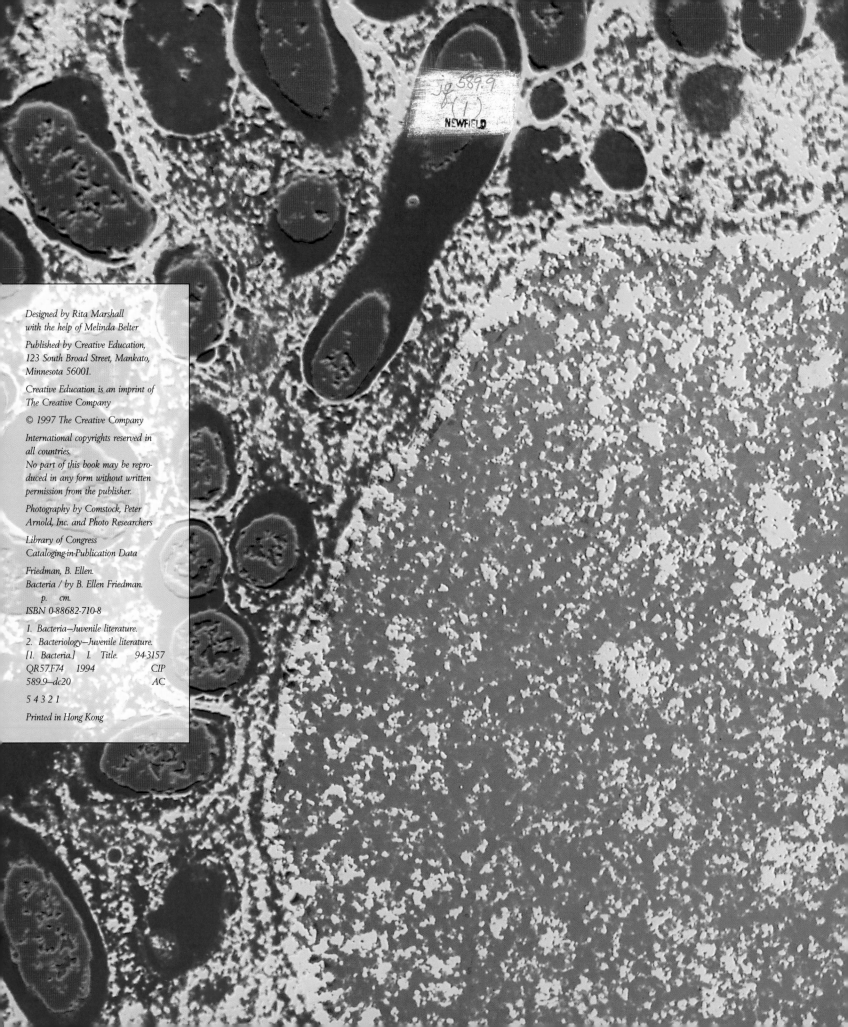

Designed by Rita Marshall
with the help of Melinda Belter

Published by Creative Education,
123 South Broad Street, Mankato,
Minnesota 56001.

Creative Education is an imprint of
The Creative Company

Photography by Comstock, Peter
Arnold, Inc. and Photo Researchers

Library of Congress
Cataloging-in-Publication Data

Friedman, B. Ellen.
Bacteria / by B. Ellen Friedman.
    p.   cm.
ISBN 0-88682-710-8

1. Bacteria—Juvenile literature.
2. Bacteriology—Juvenile literature.
[1. Bacteria]   I. Title.   94-3157
QR57.F74   1994   CIP
589.9—dc20   AC

5 4 3 2 1

Printed in Hong Kong

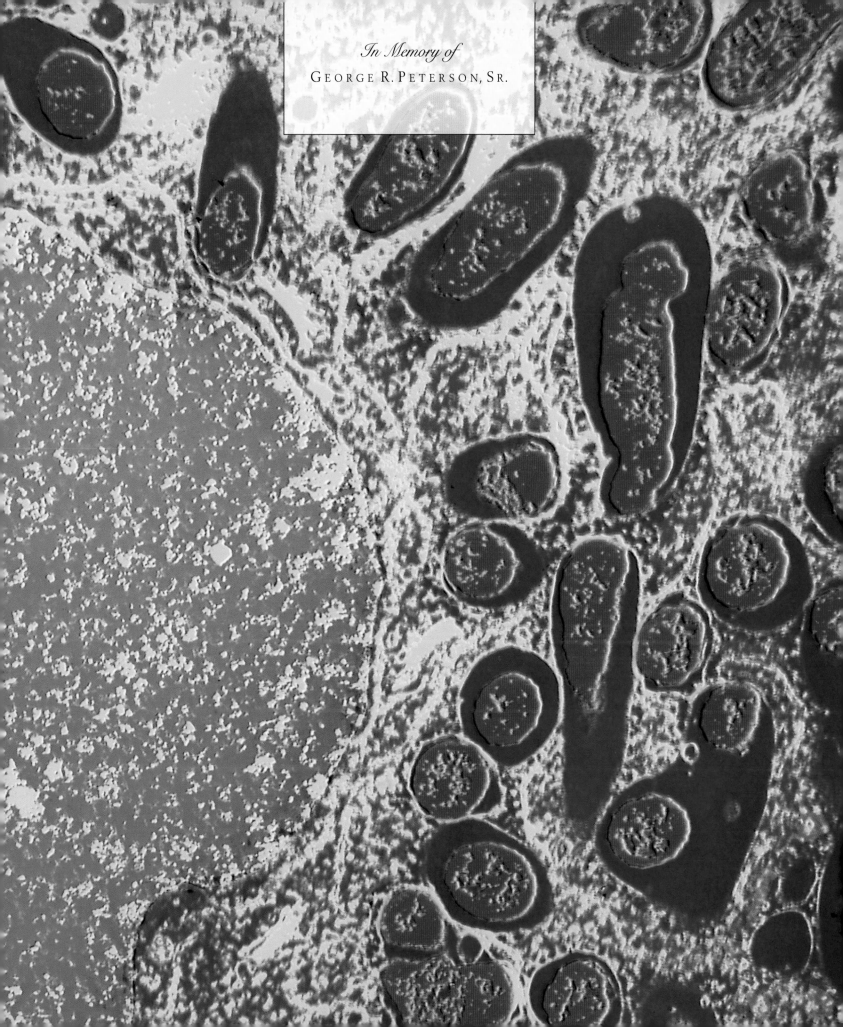

Most people think of bacteria as tiny germs that cause disease. They're right—to an extent. Bacteria are very small. One bacterium is generally about one-tenth the size of a single human red blood cell. Many bacteria cause disease, but what most people don't know is that bacteria also contribute to our world in countless positive ways. Some actually fight disease; others create and enrich the soil. Still others are used to make food. So, while *Bacteria* are sometimes our competitors in life, they are always our partners.

Bacteria are found everywhere: in the frozen interior of Antarctica, in the salty waters of the Great Salt Lake in Utah, in the boiling hot springs of Yellowstone, and in the depths of the ocean. They reside in the air, in the soil, and in our bodies. In fact, these simple

Cocci, *tooth bacteria.*

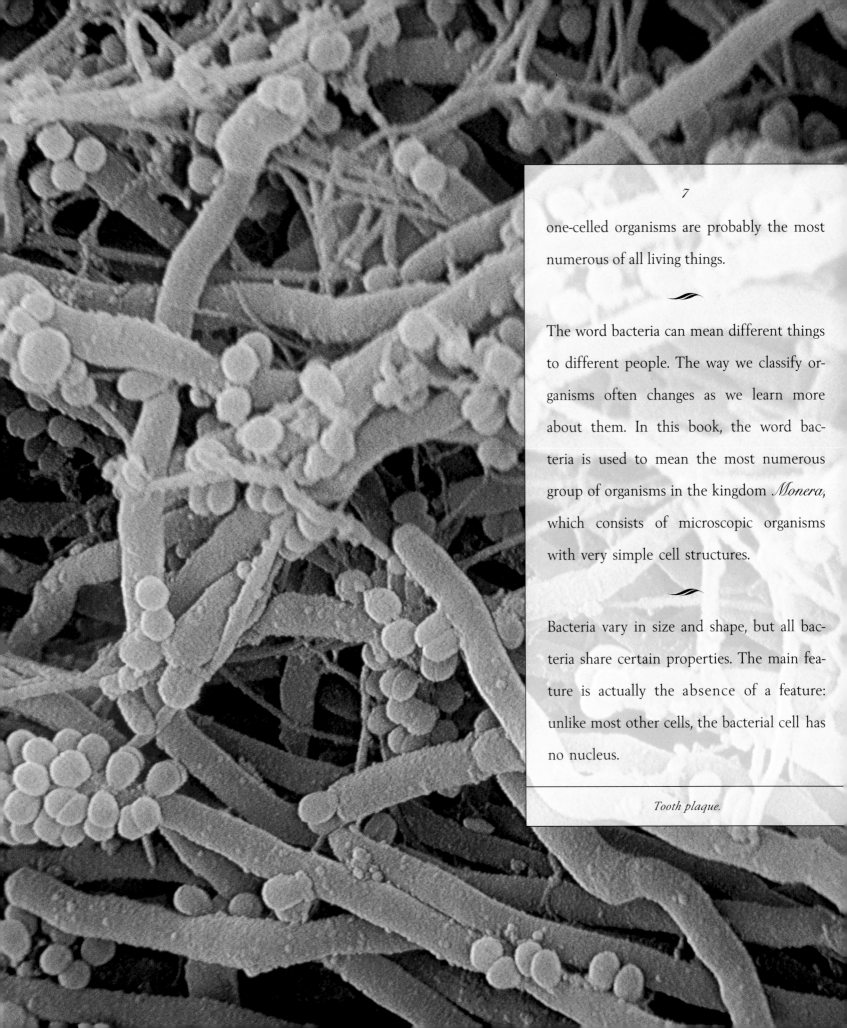

one-celled organisms are probably the most numerous of all living things.

—

The word bacteria can mean different things to different people. The way we classify organisms often changes as we learn more about them. In this book, the word bacteria is used to mean the most numerous group of organisms in the kingdom *Monera*, which consists of microscopic organisms with very simple cell structures.

—

Bacteria vary in size and shape, but all bacteria share certain properties. The main feature is actually the absence of a feature: unlike most other cells, the bacterial cell has no nucleus.

Tooth plaque.

A cell can be thought of as a "living room" enclosed by a membrane. Trillions of cells make up the bodies of plants or animals. Each of these cells has additional compartments inside. One of these compartments, the *Nucleus*, contains genetic material that has the instructions for all cell activities. This genetic material is called deoxyribonucleic acid or *DNA*. But there is no nucleus in a bacterial cell; instead, its DNA floats free as an elaborate coil. Most bacterial cells are protected on the outside by a rigid cell wall, similar to that found in plant cells. A few types of bacteria, however, have no cell walls.

Streptococcus pneumoniae, *common cause of pneumonia.*

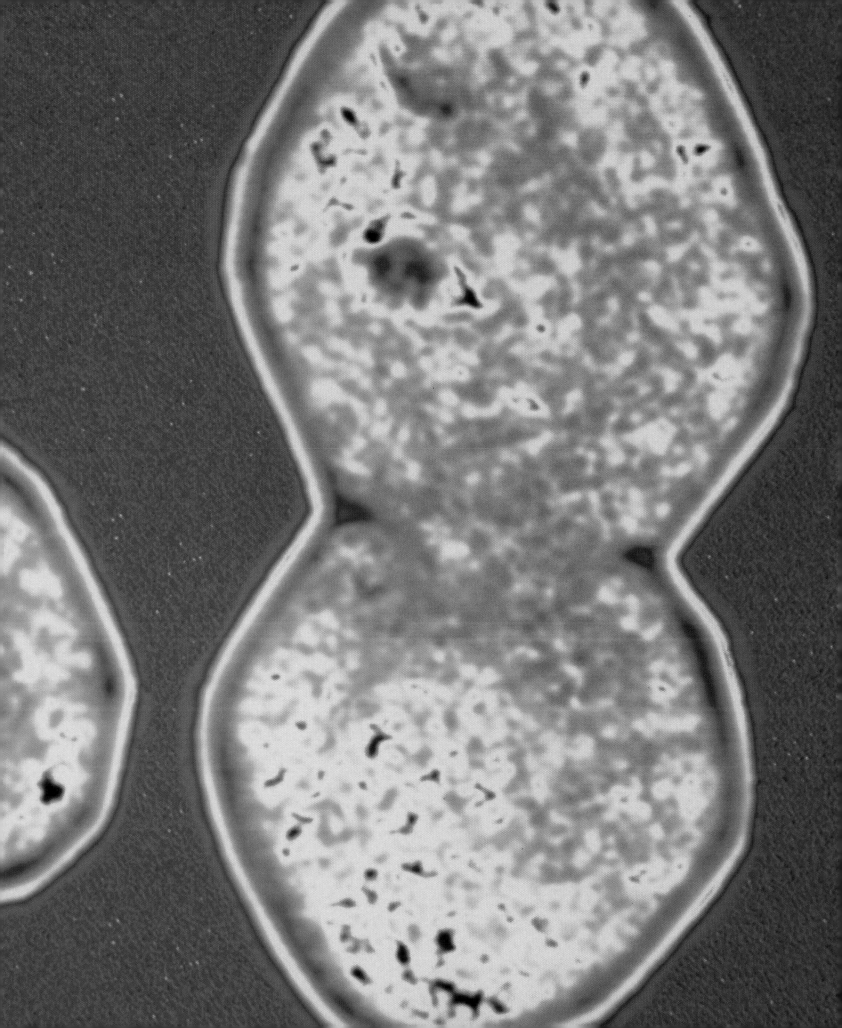

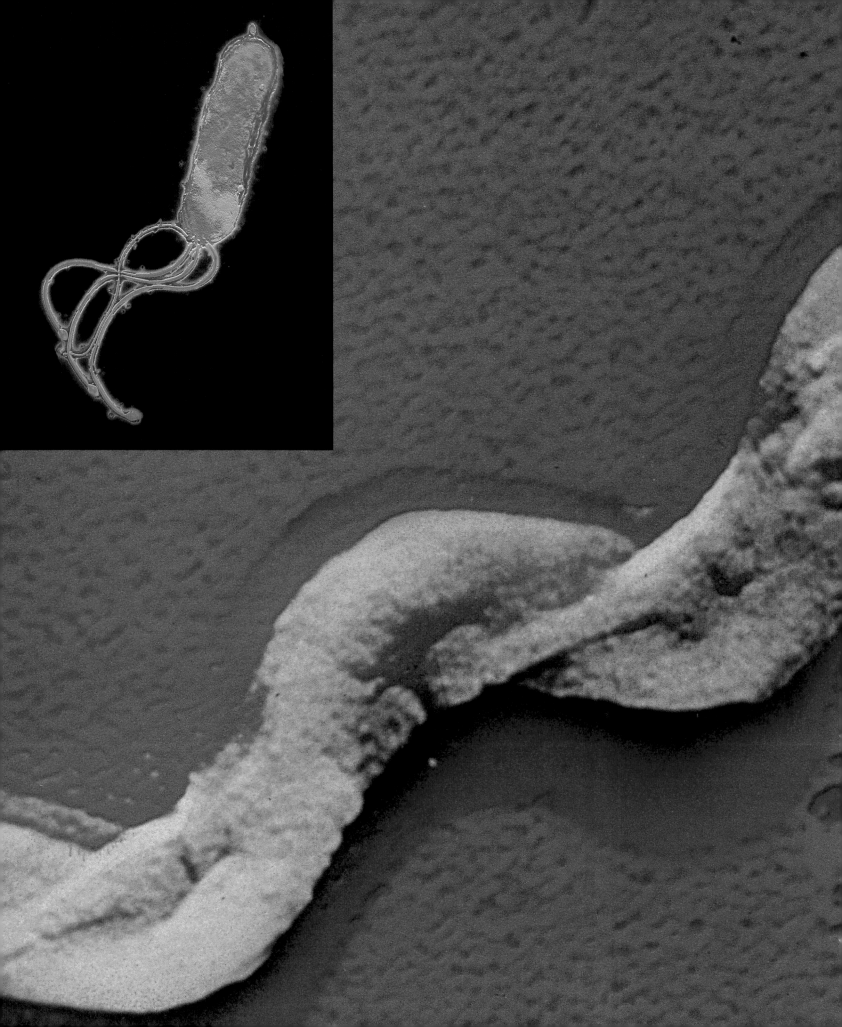

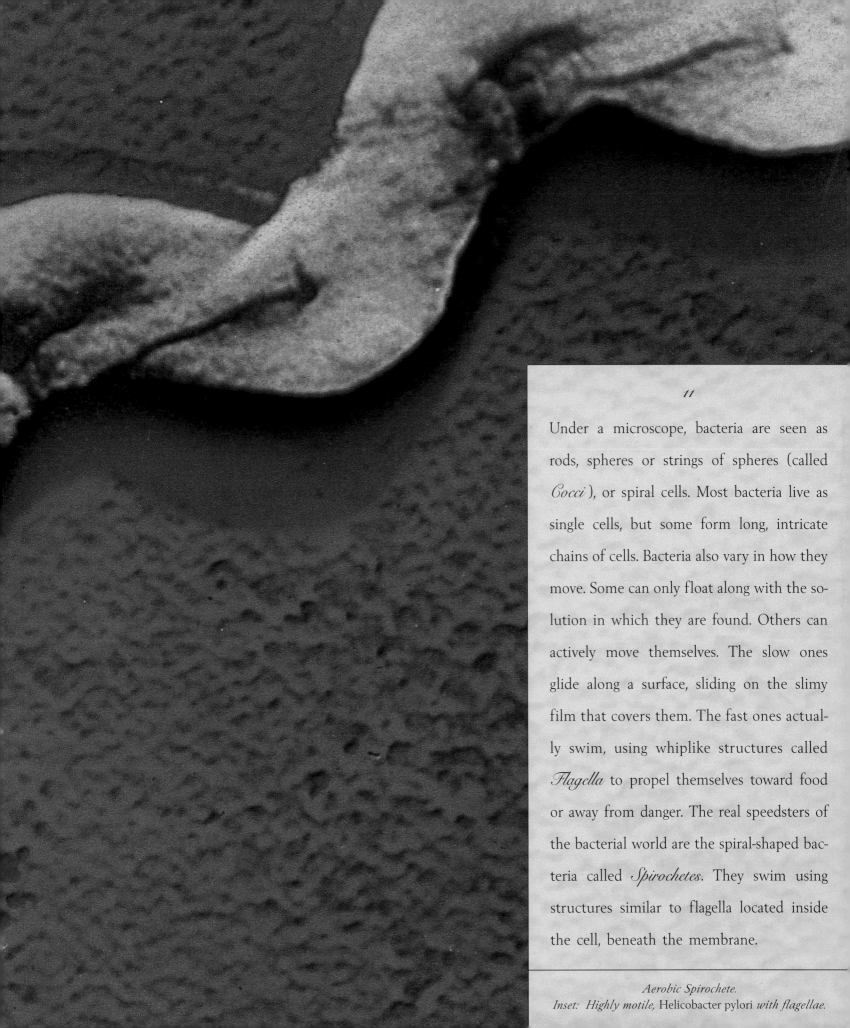

Under a microscope, bacteria are seen as rods, spheres or strings of spheres (called *Cocci*), or spiral cells. Most bacteria live as single cells, but some form long, intricate chains of cells. Bacteria also vary in how they move. Some can only float along with the solution in which they are found. Others can actively move themselves. The slow ones glide along a surface, sliding on the slimy film that covers them. The fast ones actually swim, using whiplike structures called *Flagella* to propel themselves toward food or away from danger. The real speedsters of the bacterial world are the spiral-shaped bacteria called *Spirochetes*. They swim using structures similar to flagella located inside the cell, beneath the membrane.

Aerobic Spirochete.
Inset: Highly motile, Helicobacter pylori *with flagellae.*

Bacteria can be present in huge numbers in a small area. One square centimeter of healthy human skin is home to tens of thousands of bacteria. Even the air we breathe may have more than 100 bacteria per cubic foot. Their abundance is largely the result of their ability to reproduce rapidly. Bacteria reproduce in a process called *Fission*, or simple division. In ideal circumstances, bacteria can divide as quickly as once every 20 minutes. If you started with 20 bacteria cells, in one hour they would become 160 cells. In another hour, there would be nearly 1,300 cells. By the end of the third hour, the original 20 bacteria would have produced more than 10,200 cells. If such a thing happened with humans, the number of students in a class-room would increase to fill a sports stadium in just three hours! Usually, however, the level of bacterial growth is limited by the food supply and the amount of space available.

Different types of bacteria grow in very different conditions. Some bacteria, called *Anaerobes*, grow in the absence of oxygen. Others, called *Aerobes*, can grow where oxygen is present, even using it much as we do. Many bacteria thrive in extreme conditions—in the nearly boiling, acidic waters of hot springs, for example, or in the salty water of the Great Salt Lake in Utah.

Salmonella cell dividing.

The process of using energy from the sun to power reactions that make food is called *Photosynthesis*. Plants do this, giving off oxygen as a waste product. Some anaerobic bacteria do something very similar, although no oxygen is released. Called photosynthetic bacteria, they contain several colored pigments that trap energy from sunlight. Green sulfur bacteria, purple sulfur bacteria, and purple nonsulfur bacteria are examples of photosynthetic bacteria.

Within the Monera kingdom, however, are photosynthetic organisms that do give off oxygen as a waste product. They are called *Cyanobacteria*, and they are close relatives of the general bacteria. Scientists believe that, billions of years ago, early forms of cyanobacteria produced the oxygen in the earth's atmosphere.

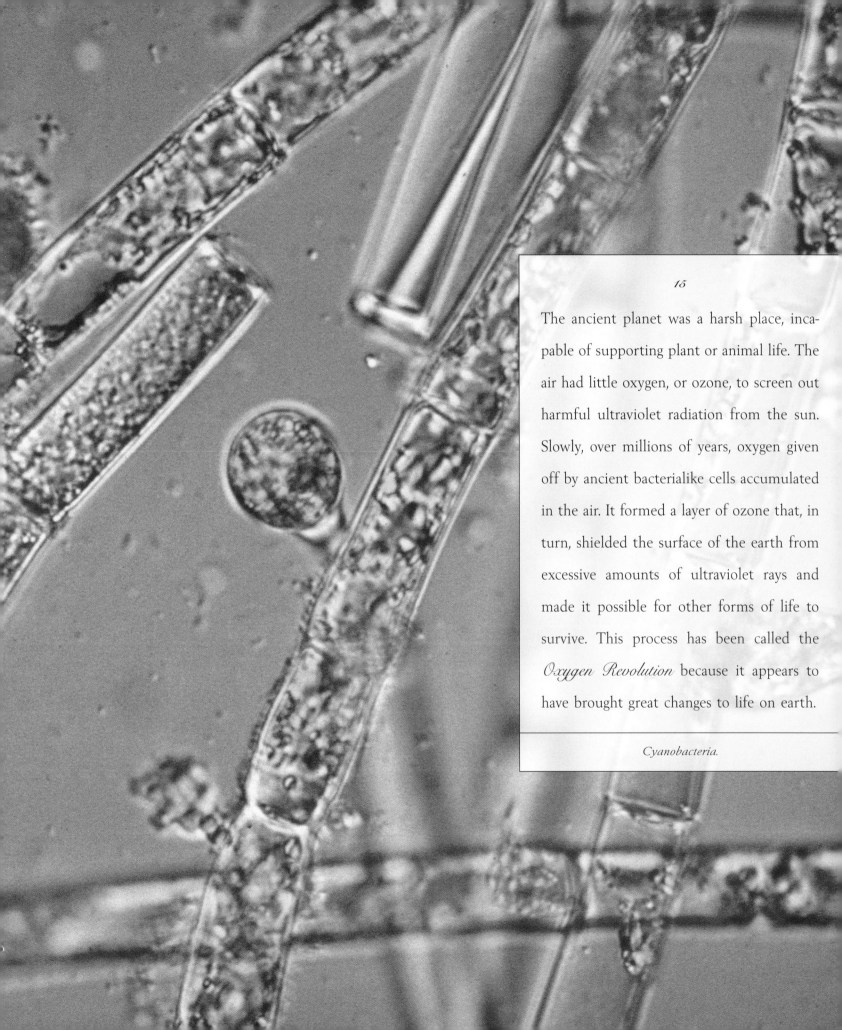

The ancient planet was a harsh place, incapable of supporting plant or animal life. The air had little oxygen, or ozone, to screen out harmful ultraviolet radiation from the sun. Slowly, over millions of years, oxygen given off by ancient bacterialike cells accumulated in the air. It formed a layer of ozone that, in turn, shielded the surface of the earth from excessive amounts of ultraviolet rays and made it possible for other forms of life to survive. This process has been called the *Oxygen Revolution* because it appears to have brought great changes to life on earth.

Cyanobacteria.

Modern bacteria, too, are essential to life on our planet, carrying out important chemical activities that affect all other forms of life. For instance, bacteria make up over 95 percent of the microorganisms living in the soil. But bacteria don't just live in soil, they actually help create it. Soil consists of tiny rocks, minerals, water, and *Humus*, which is organic material from dead plants and animals. Bacteria known as *Decomposers* break down the humus into simple materials that can be reused by living things.

Another group of bacteria makes nitrogen available to living things. Soil bacteria in the genus *Rhizobium* fix nitrogen gas from the air into a usable form as a kind of natural fertilizer. These bacteria live inside knobs on the roots of plants such as peas and alfalfa.

Rhizobium leguminosarum, *free living soil bacterium.*

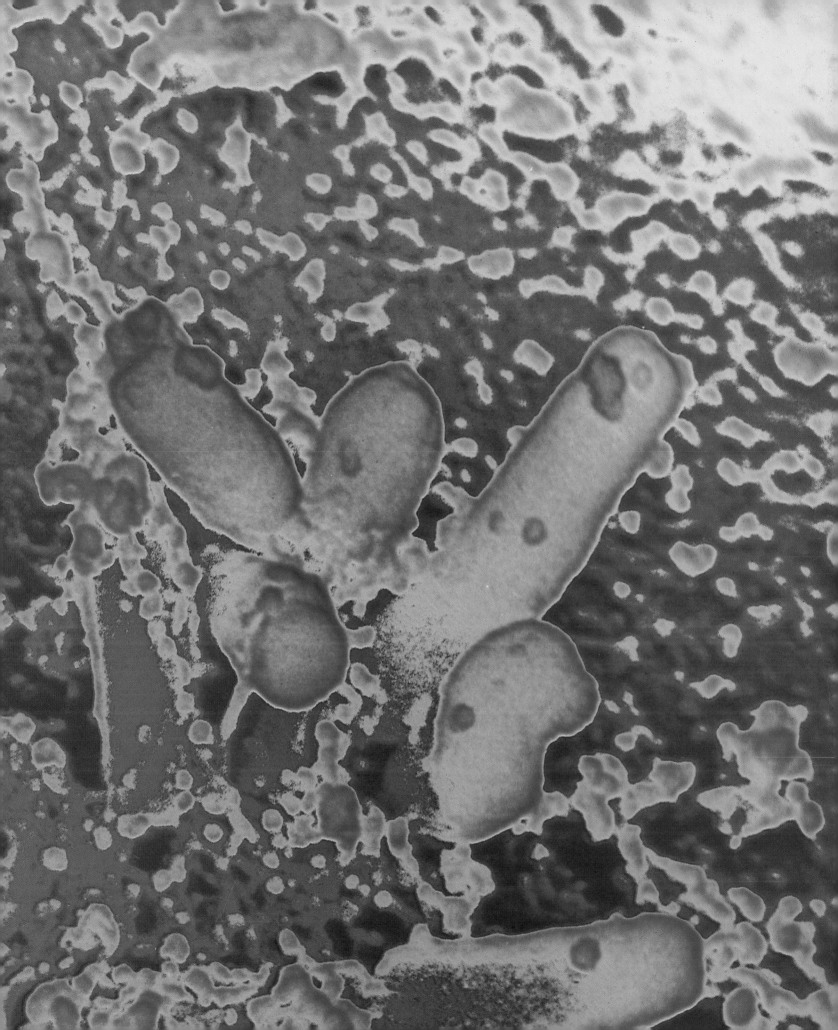

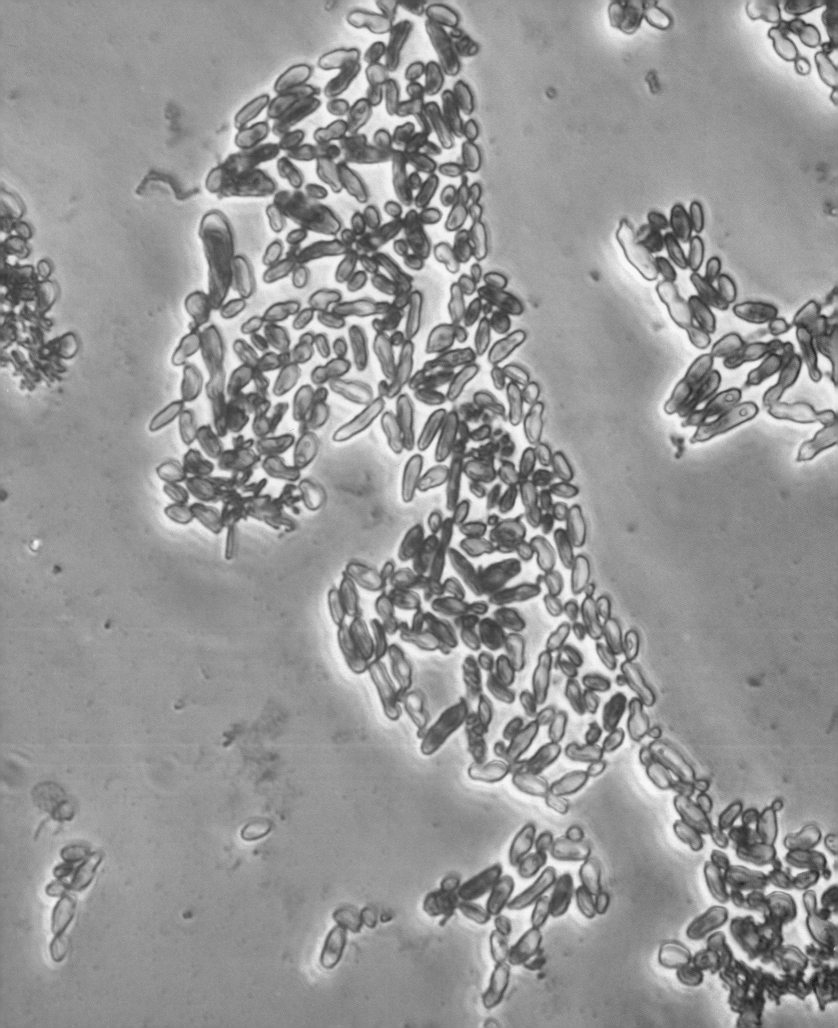

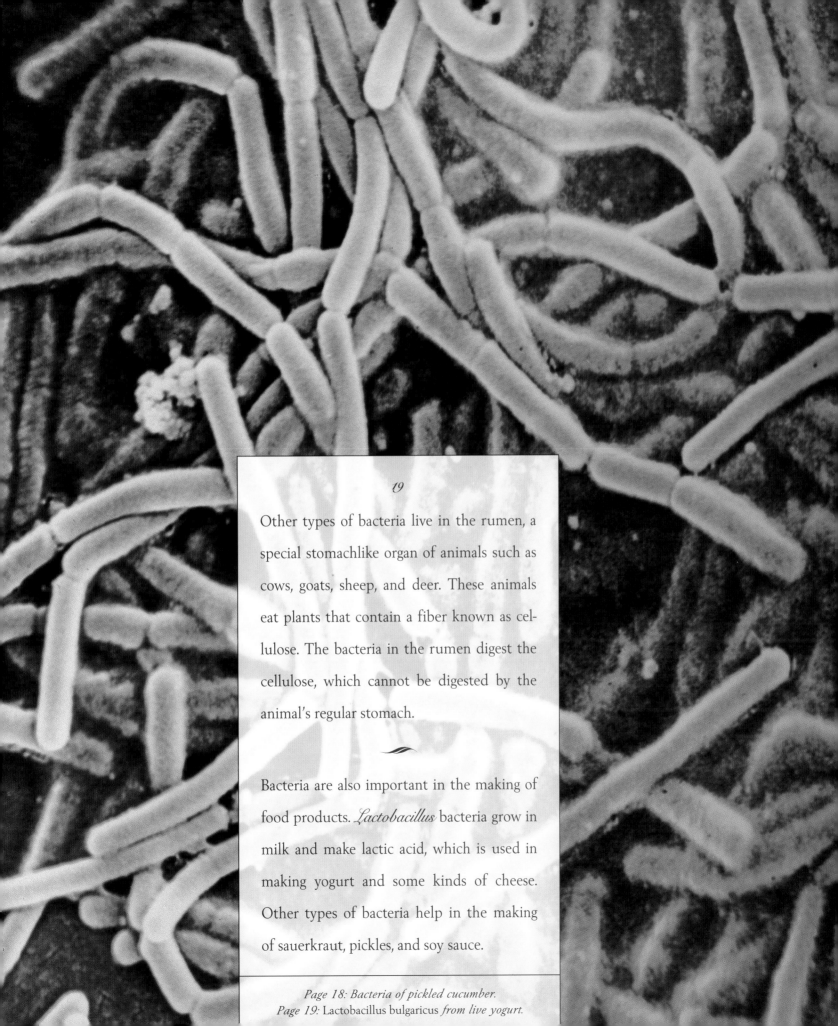

19

Other types of bacteria live in the rumen, a special stomachlike organ of animals such as cows, goats, sheep, and deer. These animals eat plants that contain a fiber known as cellulose. The bacteria in the rumen digest the cellulose, which cannot be digested by the animal's regular stomach.

Bacteria are also important in the making of food products. *Lactobacillus* bacteria grow in milk and make lactic acid, which is used in making yogurt and some kinds of cheese. Other types of bacteria help in the making of sauerkraut, pickles, and soy sauce.

Page 18: Bacteria of pickled cucumber.
Page 19: Lactobacillus bulgaricus *from live yogurt.*

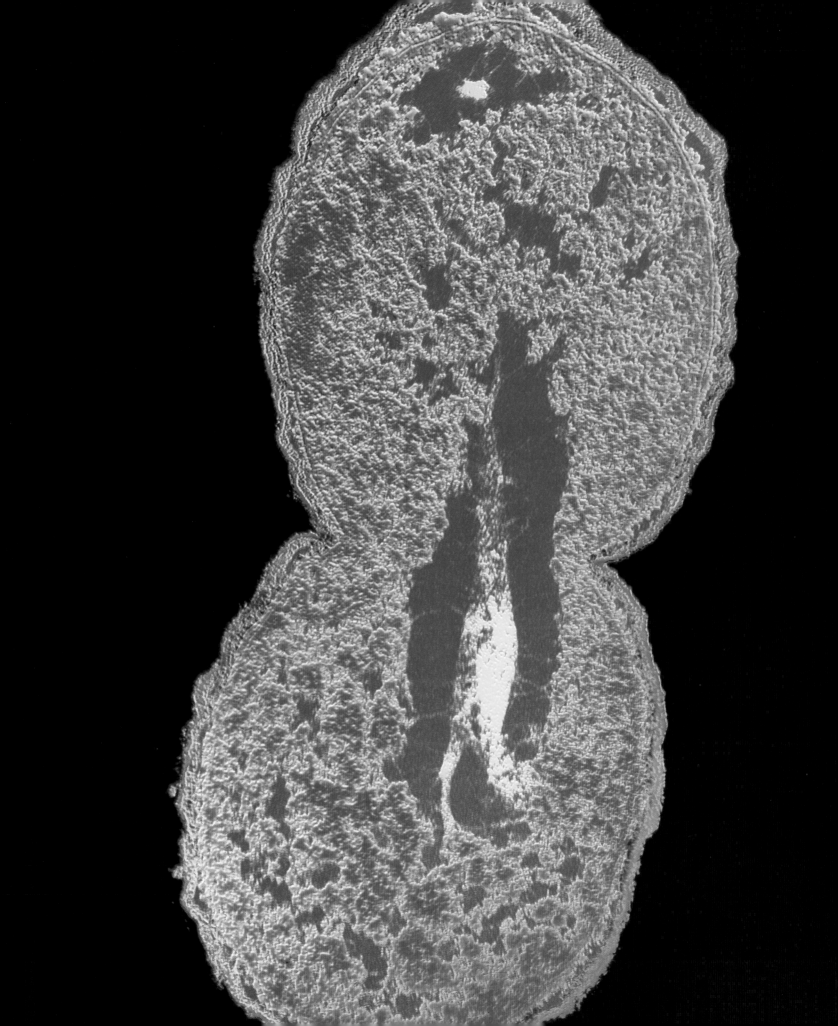

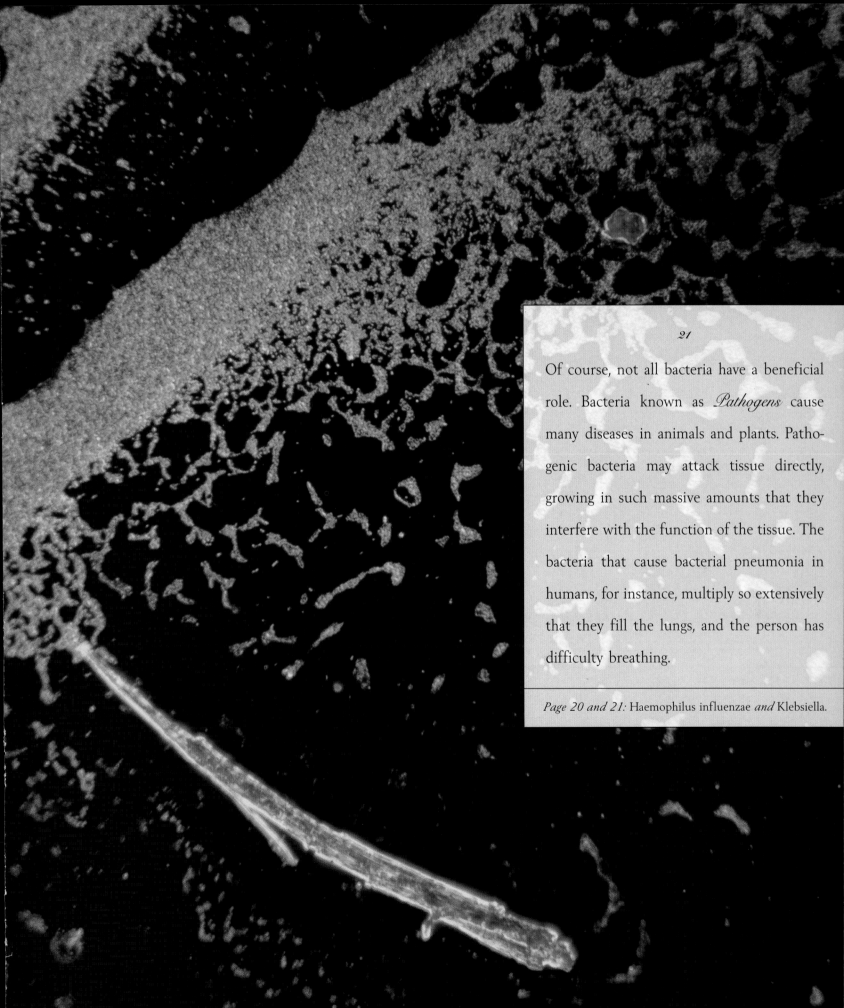

Of course, not all bacteria have a beneficial role. Bacteria known as *Pathogens* cause many diseases in animals and plants. Pathogenic bacteria may attack tissue directly, growing in such massive amounts that they interfere with the function of the tissue. The bacteria that cause bacterial pneumonia in humans, for instance, multiply so extensively that they fill the lungs, and the person has difficulty breathing.

Page 20 and 21: Haemophilus influenzae *and* Klebsiella.

Other pathogenic bacteria produce *Toxins*, chemicals that can damage the body's systems and cause illness or even death. The *Haemophilus* bacteria make a toxin that breaks apart red blood cells. Some species of *Haemophilus* cause conjunctivitis (pink eye), certain strains of flu and meningitis, and whooping cough. A more common infection caused by bacteria is acne, which produces blemishes on the skin in about 80 percent of all people. An increase in normal skin oils during teenage years can lead to acne. Tiny openings in the skin become plugged by these oils. Bacteria build up there, using the oils as a food source and causing acne sores.

Chlamydia trachomatis *causes pinkeye and blindness.*

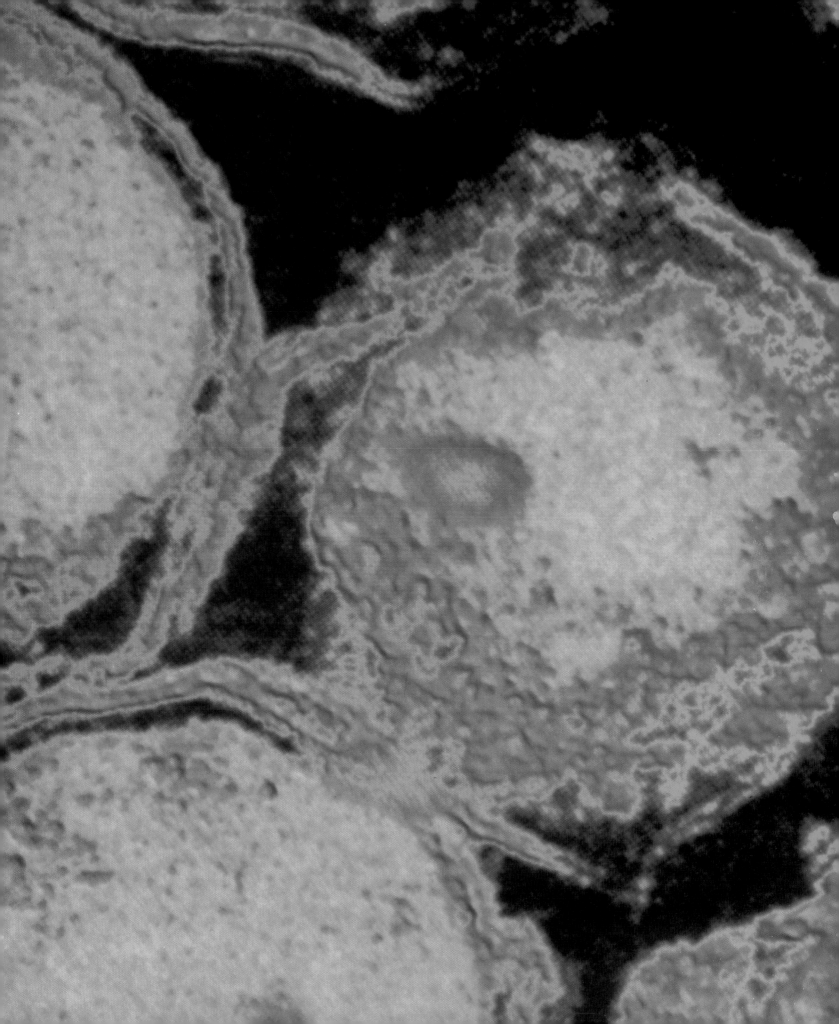

A particularly deadly group of toxin-producing bacteria are the *Clostridium* bacteria. One species, C. *tetani*, grows in deep puncture wounds that are not cleaned properly. Once inside a wound, the pathogen makes a paralytic nerve toxin that causes tetanus—a painful and often fatal disease that is preventable through vaccination. Yet another species, C. *botulinum*, can contaminate improperly canned food. If a person eats contaminated food without cooking it, botulism food poison will occur and may result in death. Cooking the food before eating it, however, destroys the toxin.

Clostridium botulinum.

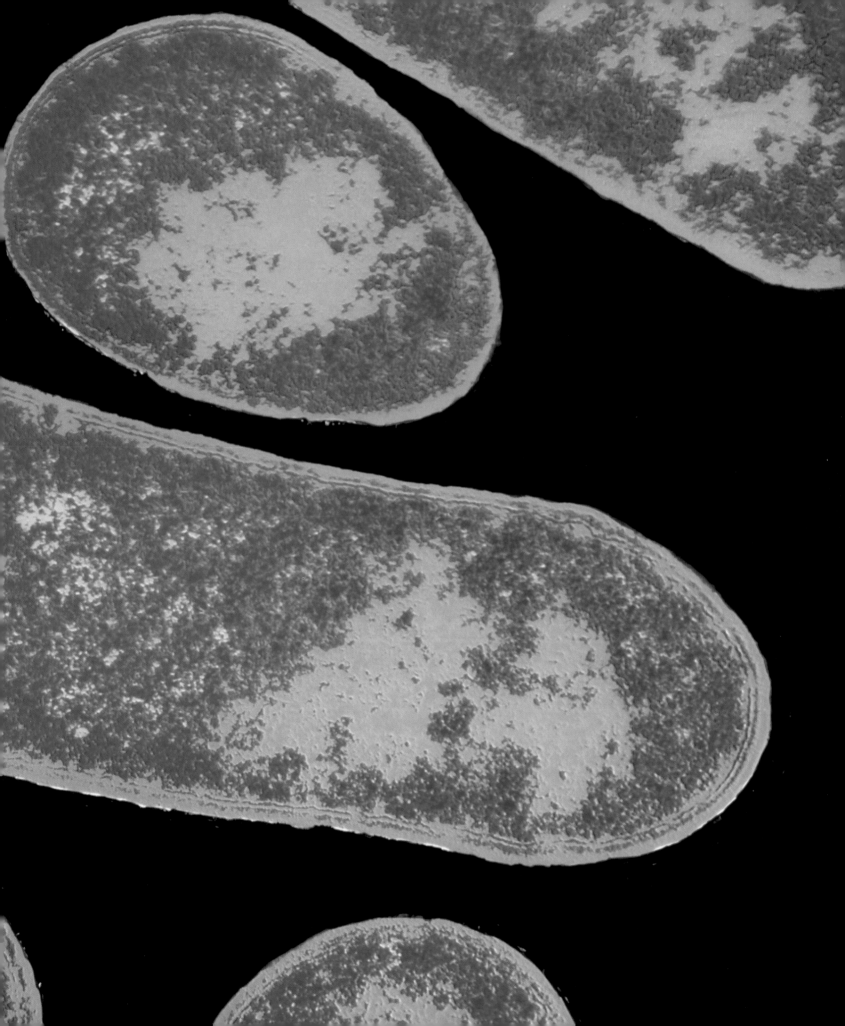

Some bacteria may also cause harm through *Putrefaction*, the decomposition of tissue. Gangrene, an extremely dangerous infection, can be caused by *Clostridium perfringens* bacteria that decompose the tissue of the body.

———

Bacteria also live inside cells as *Parasites*, where they depend on the host cell to live. They often cause harm to the host organism. *Rickettsia* are very tiny bacteria that cause typhus fever and spotted fever in humans. *Mycoplasma* cause some types of pneumonia and sexually transmitted diseases in people. They also cause a disease of orange trees. Mycoplasma are unusual in that they lack a cell wall.

Clostridium perfringens.

Most bacteria are not pathogenic. In fact, many bacteria are useful in fighting disease. Some types of bacteria reside in or on the body and keep the pathogens from growing. In addition, some bacteria are used to make *Antibiotics*, medicines that are taken for bacterial infections. Bacteria in the genus *Streptomyces*, for instance, make over 500 types of antibiotic medicine. Antibiotics kill bacteria without hurting human cells. But they can sometimes kill beneficial bacteria as well, and so they must be used with care.

Staphylococcus epidermidis.

One species of bacteria that is particularly useful to humans is the *Escherichia coli*, a common bacteria that lives in the human digestive tract. *E. coli* is a rod-shaped bacteria that is one of the most studied organisms on earth. Because it is easily grown in a laboratory and not especially dangerous, it became the subject of early experiments in the study of bacteria and cell biology. Later, because there was so much information available, it was used as a test subject in much more complex experiments.

❦

Today *E. coli* has become even more important to scientists, because it is one of the major bacterial hosts in genetic engineering.

Scientists have learned how to transfer genes from one species to another, and even build new combinations of genes in the laboratory. Many of the manipulations of genetic material are carried out in tiny test tubes. Then the new genes are put inside a living organism to make many copies. *E. coli* is usually used as a host in these gene transfers. These techniques are already producing new medicines. *Insulin* is an important human protein used to treat the disease called diabetes. Now it can be made in giant vats, produced by special bacteria that have been genetically altered to carry the human gene for insulin.

Plasmids of bacterial DNA from E. coli.

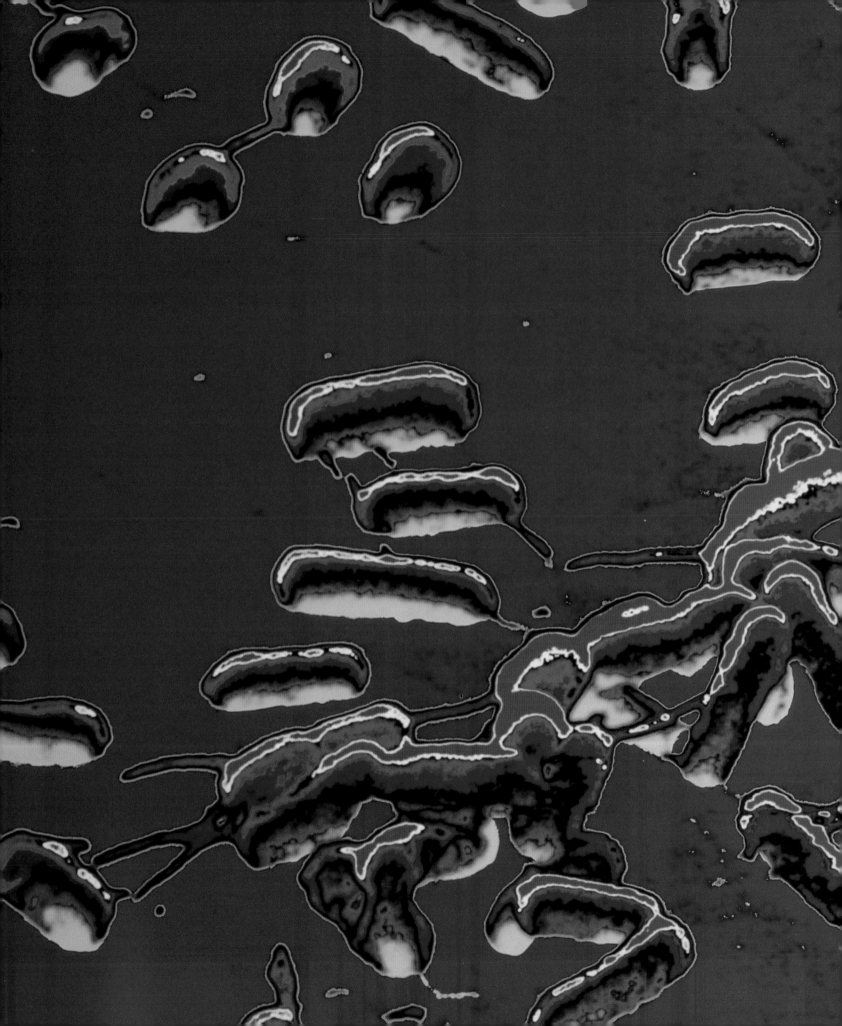

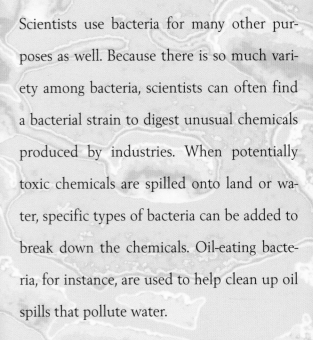

Scientists use bacteria for many other purposes as well. Because there is so much variety among bacteria, scientists can often find a bacterial strain to digest unusual chemicals produced by industries. When potentially toxic chemicals are spilled onto land or water, specific types of bacteria can be added to break down the chemicals. Oil-eating bacteria, for instance, are used to help clean up oil spills that pollute water.

Since ancient times, bacteria have influenced the biological and chemical aspects of our planet. Their ability to reproduce quickly, use many types of food sources, and withstand a wide variety of conditions has placed them among the most successful of all living organisms. But we are just beginning to understand their importance as our partners in life. With the technologies of modern science, we continue to learn about the properties of bacteria that make them so successful at survival. This once unseen kingdom of organisms has been revealed as a fascinating array of living things.

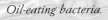

Oil-eating bacteria.

Index